Due
APRIC 23

Learning About Your Health

Tonsillitis

By

Kenneth T. Burles

ROURKE PRESS, INC.
VERO BEACH, FLORIDA 32964

© 1998 Rourke Press, Inc.

Printed in the United States of America.

Library of Congress Cataloging-in-Publication Data

Burles, Kenneth T., 1946-
    Tonsillitis/Kenneth T. Burles.
    p.   cm. — (Learning about your health)
Includes index.
Summary: Discusses the nature, causes, and treatment of tonsillitis and other kinds of sore throats.
    ISBN 1-57103-257-6
    1. Tonsillitis — Juvenile literature. 2. Tonsils—Juvenile literature. [1. Tonsillitis. 2. Tonsils 3. Throat—Diseases.]
I. Title. II. Series: Burles, Kenneth T., 1946-   Learning about your health.
RF491.887   1998
616.3'14—dc21   98-22381
                                                                                          CIP
                                                                                           AC

Photographs: Cover, © Digital Stock; pp. 5, 9, 13, 15, 17, 23, © PhotoDisc; pp. 11, 21, 25, © Adobe Systems Incorporated.

Illustrations by Paul Calderon.

Contents

Ouch!

Your throat hurts when you swallow. Your head aches. You have a fever. Your neck is swollen. It hurts right behind your jaw bone. You have a very sore throat. You might have **tonsillitis** (**tawn**-sill-eye-tus).

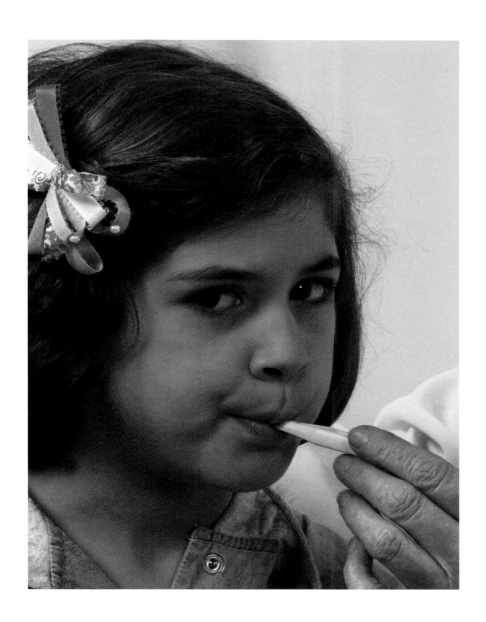

What is Tonsillitis?

Tonsillitis is the infection of your **tonsils** (**tawn**-sills). The tonsils are located in the back of your mouth on each side of your throat. They fight germs that are trying to infect the nose or throat. They are larger in children than in adults. They are an important part of your **immune** (im-**youn**) **system**.

Tonsils swell because they are fighting **infection** (in-**feck**-shun. The swelling may

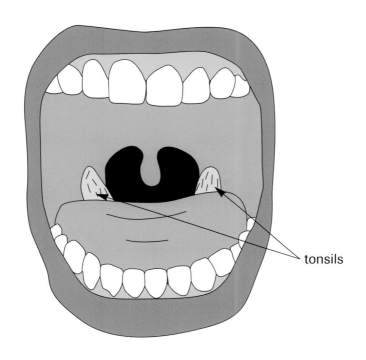

tonsils

make it hard to swallow. If they become
too large, it becomes hard to breathe. If the
swelling does not go down in a couple of
days, you must see a doctor.

What Will the Doctor Do?

The doctor can look in your mouth and see how swollen your tonsils are. He also can take a throat culture, a sample of the germs in your mouth. The test will tell him if your tonsillitis is caused by **bacteria** (back-**tear**-e-uh) or a **virus** (**vy**-russ).

If the cause is bacteria, he can prescribe powerful medicines called **antibiotics** (anti-bi-**ot**-icks) to kill the bacteria. After a few days, you will feel better. You will still continue to take the antibiotics until they are all gone. If the cause is a virus, you must wait for your body to fight off the virus.

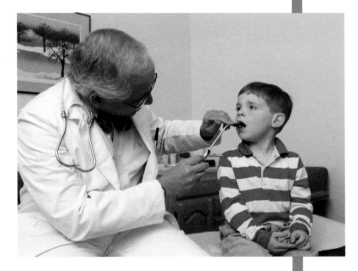

The doctor looks in your mouth to check for swollen tonsils.

How Do Viruses and Bacteria Get in My Body?

Viruses and bacteria are very tiny organisms (**or**-gahn-isms) They travel through air, water, food, or touch. Insects can carry them and infect you with a bite. They are the enemy of the immune system.

We can be **vaccinated** (**vack**-sin-ate-ed) for some viruses and bacteria. A small dose of a virus is given to you by a shot. The body fights the small dose. The next time the body sees the virus it fights it and you do not become sick. This is called vaccination. Scientists look for **vaccines** and medicines against viruses that now kill many people such as AIDS and cancer.

Are Tonsils Necessary?

In the past, people did not think tonsils were important. If a child had tonsillitis frequently, the doctor would remove the tonsils. Now, we know that they are especially important for children up to about age 12.

The discovery of antibiotics has made it easier to treat tonsillitis in children. Even if

Tonsillitis can be treated with antibiotics.

a child has tonsillitis two or three times a year, the doctor will not remove the tonsils. If a child reaches the age of twelve and has tonsillitis three or four times a year, the doctor might say the child has **chronic** (**krahn**-ick) **tonsillitis.**

Tonsillectomy. When?

The doctor will recommend a **tonsillectomy** (tawn-sill-**eckt**-ah-me) for the child with chronic tonsillitis. He will schedule **surgery** (**sir**-jer-e) to remove the tonsils. When they are removed, the tonsils will not grow back.

A tonsillectomy is done in a hospital. The child whose tonsils are being removed is called a **patient** (**pay**-shunt). He is given **anesthesia** (ann-ah-**sthee**-see-ah) to put

You need to stay at the hospital when you have a tonsillectomy.

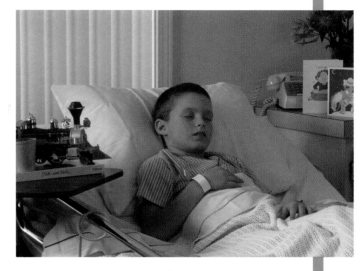

him to sleep so he will not feel the surgery. He will not be awake during the surgery. The doctor cuts away the tissue in the back of the throat. It would be uncomfortable for the patient to feel the surgery.

After the surgery, the doctor will check the patient. If there are no problems, the patient can go home.

How Will the Patient Feel?

After a tonsillectomy, the patient's throat will feel very sore. Swallowing liquids will even be hard. He will not be able to swallow solid foods. Soon, the patient will begin to eat soft foods and liquids. The more he swallows, the less it will hurt.

Ice cream, jello, and pudding are good foods to eat after a tonsillectomy. Cool drinks also will make the throat start to feel better. It will take about two weeks before the sore feeling in the throat goes away.

The Mouth
and Throat

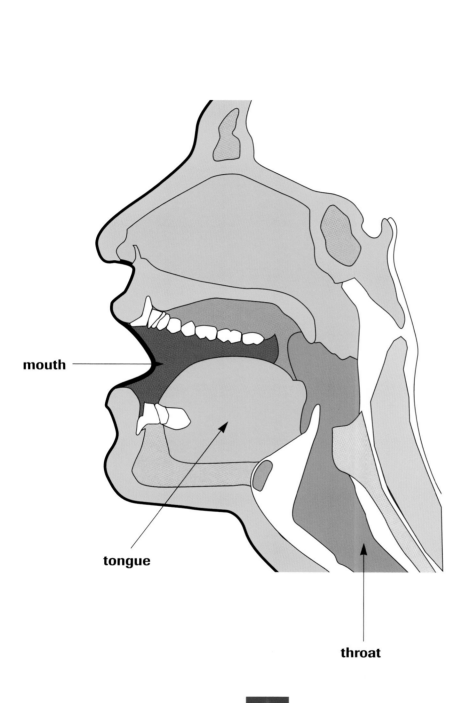

mouth

tongue

throat

Sore Throat

A sore throat can be caused by many things. It usually is not as serious as tonsillitis and will go away in a few days to a week. Many sore throats are caused by infections in the ears and nose. The infections can be caused by viruses or bacteria. Bacteria can be treated with antibiotics. Viruses cannot be treated. The body's immune system must fight the virus.

Streptococcus (strep-tah-**cock**-cuss) is the most common cause of sore throats and tonsillitis. People often visit the doctor to find out if they have "strep" throat, or are infected with streptococcus. Antibiotics will kill the streptococcus.

Antibiotics come in syrup or pill form.

What Do I Do for a Sore Throat?

Stay home and rest when you have a sore throat. You can gargle with a mix of salt and water to make your throat feel better. You can take medicine to reduce your fever. Inhaling steam or sucking on a **menthol lozenge** may make your throat feel better for a short time.

Soup is a good food to eat when you have a sore throat.

You will not want to eat much food because swallowing will hurt. You can drink cool drinks, eat puddings or ice cream, and have a bowl of soup.

I Lost
My Voice!

An infection of the voice box may result in **laryngitis** (lare-in-**ji**-tis). The voice box is called the **larynx** (**lare**-inks). If a virus infects the voice box, you will become **hoarse** (horse). Soon, you will open your mouth to speak but only air or a whisper will come out.

Lozenges can relieve sore throat pain.

If you "lose your voice" it is best not to talk. You must wait a few days until the virus passes. You should drink soothing liquids and suck on throat lozenges.

The Immune System

The body's immune system fights germs that try to get into the body. Many parts of the body play a role in the immune system. They must all work together to keep the body free of disease.

The tonsils are part of the **lymphatic** (limp-**fat**-ick) **system**. They are lymph nodes, or glands. This system helps to collect fluids in the body and return them to the bloodstream. The lymphatic system works with the **circulatory** (**sir**-cue-lah-tor-e) **system** to kill germs. There are red blood cells and white blood cells. The white cells surround the invaders and kill them.

The immune system has a memory. Once it battles a germ, it learns how to fight off the infection the next time it meets that germ.

Glossary

anesthesia (ann-ah-**sthee**-see-ah) - something that puts you to sleep.

antibiotics (anti-bi-**ot**-icks) - medicines that kill bacteria.

bacteria (back-**tear**-e-uh) - germs that infect the body.

chronic (**krahn**-ick) - an illness that will not go away.

circulatory (**sir**-cue-lah-tor-e) system - parts of the body that move blood.

hoarse (**horse**) - to have a rough, low voice.

immune (im-**youn**) system - the parts of the body that fight bacteria and viruses.

infection (in-**feck**-shun) - illness caused by germs.

laryngitis (lare-in-**ji**-tis) - to lose your voice.

larynx (**lare**-inks) - the voice box.

lymphatic (limp-**fat**-ick) system - parts of the body that return fluids to the bloodstream.

menthol lozenge (**men**-thall **laws**-enj) - a cool drop you suck on to relieve throat pain.

organisms (**or**-gahn-isms) - tiny living things.

patient (**pay**-shunt) - a person who is cared for by a doctor.

streptoccus (strep-tah-**cock**-cuss) - a germ that often causes sore throat.

tonsillectomy (tawn-sill-**eckt**-ah-me) - an operation to remove the tonsils.

tonsillitis (tawn-sill-**eye**-tus) - the infection of the tonsils.

tonsils (**tawn**-sills) - glands in the back of the throat that fight germs.

vaccinate (**vack**-sin-ate) - to get a shot with a small amount of a virus.

virus (**vy**-russ) - a germ that infects the body.

For More Information

Children's Healthwatch from Mayo Clinic. http://healthfront.com

Grolier Encyclopedia of Science and Technology. Danbury, CT: Grolier Educational Corporation, 1994.

Health Infopark. http://www.merck.com

Kingfisher Children's Encyclopedia. New York: Kingfisher Books, 1992.

Raintree Steck-Vaughn Illustrated Science Encyclopedia. Austin, TX: Steck-Vaughn, 1997.

Rourke's World of Science Encyclopedia. Vero Beach, FL: Rourke Corporation, Inc., 1998.

The World Book Encyclopedia. Chicago: World Book, Inc., 1998.

Index